Henry T. Winterblossom

The Game of Draw-Poker - Mathematically Illustrated

being a complete treatise on the game, giving the prospective value of each hand before and after the draw, and the true method of discarding and drawing

Henry T. Winterblossom

The Game of Draw-Poker - Mathematically Illustrated
being a complete treatise on the game, giving the prospective value of each hand before and after the draw, and the true method of discarding and drawing

ISBN/EAN: 9783337266592

Printed in Europe, USA, Canada, Australia, Japan

THE GAME

OF

DRAW-POKER,

MATHEMATICALLY ILLUSTRATED;

G A COMPLETE TREATISE ON THE GAME, GIVING THE PROSPECTIVE VALUE OF EACH HAND BEFORE AND AFTER THE DRAW, AND THE TRUE METHOD OF DISCARDING AND DRAWING, WITH A THOROUGH ANALYSIS AND INSIGHT OF THE GAME AS PLAYED AT THE PRESENT DAY BY GENTLEMEN.

BY

HENRY T. WINTERBLOSSOM,

Professor of Mathematics.

NEW-YORK:

'M. H. MURPHY, PRINTER AND PUBLISHER.

1875.

INTRODUCTORY PREFACE

AMING, or gambling, in some form, has existed from time immemorial. If we consider the word in a pastoral sense, it will est to us the earliest efforts of the primitive savage to provide elf with food, at a period of the year when fruit and herbs could e obtained. In his various attempts to thus supply his wants, force ratagem, as the occasion demanded, was called into play. The ine of chances and the law of supply and demand were not, perhaps, ehold words with him at this period of his existence; but it will e for our purpose to believe that success or failure in his enterprise ndered in his breast emotions of a very opposite nature.

c excitement of gambling, which is nothing more than the mixed ure and pain arising from the alternation of hope and fear, success ailure, is a necessity which all men feel, though in different degrees ding to the difference of temperament. The savage who, as Taci- nforms us, will even stake himself, when everything he possessed is led away, and the blushing, nervous girl of 14, who has (to use English) "bet" her first dollar in a raffle at a Church fair, may be dered the extreme exponents of this vice. It is not our purpose rm the reader by endeavoring to prove that gambling is indigenous e human family, and that primeval man was born with a dice-box hand. Nor do we wish to emphasize the recent discovery in Cen- Africa, which goes to show that the *Troglodytes*, progenitors doubt- f Mr. Darwin, use gold tooth-picks and are experts at the game of backgammon. We wish, however, to put on record the following truism: All games of chance create a morbid appetite in those who indulge in them, in proportion to their ignorance of the mathematical basis upon which those games are constructed. This sentence, like the shake of Burleigh's head, may be too profound for the average intellect, so we will explain it.

Suppose, for instance, two persons stake a dollar on the toss of a copper, the chance of winning or losing is equal, and they might play for a week without either improving his fortune in the least. But let one of them lay $25 to one, that the other cannot call correctly the fall of the copper five times consecutively, and an extraordinary metamorphosis takes place. Instantly they are ranged in bitter antagonism. One of the contestants thus transformed becomes the "Banque," cool and determined, confident that the twenty per cent. which the conditions of the wager place in his favor will, in the long run, give him possession of all the money that may be staked on the issue. The other will be at once recognized as the infatuated dupe, whose cupidity the illusive prize has brought out in bold relief, and who will play days and even years without power to check his downward progress in the destructive current in which he is launched. Now it is not reasonable to suppose that a person will thus play against an impossibility (in a mathematical point of view) of winning, and be conscious of the fact; hence we are led to the inevitable conclusion that, in almost every instance, his infatuation with the game is in direct ratio to his ignorance of the doctrine of chances. Everybody knows that the toss of a copper is an even chance; to guess it five times running is one chance in thirty-two: therefore, in our illustration, every twenty-five dollars won costs in the long run thirty-one. Of course the toss of the copper is merely typical of games of chance generally, all of which, no matter how played or determined, owe their fascination to the insidious method of presenting to the imagination a large prize, and deftly concealing, as far as possible, the difficulty of getting it.

The reader, at this juncture, may perhaps appear anxious to know what all this has to do with the game of DRAW-POKER. We will state it in a few words.

In playing Poker, five cards are dealt to the player, which may be termed his preliminary "hand;" he examines it and if, in his judgment, it is worth the "ante" required of each one who wishes to be interested in the "pot," he puts in the necessary sum. If not, he throws up his cards. Now as each one who "stands" has the privilege of "discarding" and drawing fresh cards, equal in number to those discarded, it becomes a vital question to know what kind of hand one should stand on, and what kind he should throw up. This, of course, is the first step in our investigation of the game, and we have endeavored to make it perfectly intelligible to the reader. All the various combinations that go to make up poker hands are then analyzed, and their mathematical expectations given. We have throughout the volume laid great stress on the question of percentage, believing beyond doubt that the player who will avail himself of the advantage which certain combinations give, will, in the majority of cases, have it in his favor, and must, in the long run, win. We have pointed out also, in a clear manner, the numerous pit-holes into which the amateur, as a rule, invariably stumbles; nor indeed is every one who thinks himself a proficient in the game, entirely free from such mishaps. Under ordinary circumstances, many years of experience and close observation, are absolutely required to perfect the student in navigating the intricate passages that are always encountered in the game. This, it is unnecessary to say, is not the least expensive part of his apprenticeship. It has therefore been our object, in preparing this volume, to keep steadily in view the principle of conservatism; and while this course may perhaps in a limited degree be open to the charge of timidity, no one will regret in the end having pursued it. The most brilliant play is rarely satisfactory when it terminates in a loss. We have used our best efforts to circumscribe, within moderate bounds, the amount of money that should be involved in any one hand. Draw-

Poker, unfortunately, is one of the few games that cannot be played so as to afford any pleasure, without the interchange of money. Indeed one might as well go on a gunning expedition with blank-cartridge, as to play Poker for "fun."

In concluding these prefatory remarks, it may be looked upon as an omission if no reference be made to an important element in the game known as "Bluffing." In former days, when the betting was unlimited, this was frequently the determining feature of a hand, no matter what the cards were; and to bluff an opponent, while holding yourself "nary pair," was the pinnacle of ambition at which all players aimed. In modern Poker however, bluffing is secondary in consequence of the numerous restrictions which are imposed on it. Notwithstanding, in the hands of a judicious player, it will always remain a power that must, under no circumstances, be slighted. To convey to the reader an adequate conception of precisely what it is and how and when it is to be used, would necessitate the invention of a new language, more copious and communicative than our present mother tongue. We have nevertheless, at various points throughout the volume, given hints as to its use, trusting to the skill and experience of the reader to thoroughly develop it as occasion demands.

All calculations that appertain to Draw-Poker hands are necessarily approximate; and the degree of approximation is determined by the nature of the combination presented,—some admitting of nearly strict accuracy, others, again, being extremely variable. The early mathematicians, Galileo, Cardan, Huyghens, and Bernoulli had to deal chiefly with dice, the combinations of which admit of positive solutions. These eminent men considered it a public duty to analyze and publish to the world the results of their investigations. In England, the appearance of Simpson's Laws of Chance was more effectual in curbing the desire for gambling than all the essays that had, up to that period, been written against it. In France, while gambling was legalized, the government had every game of chance examined by mathematical experts, and the per centage in favor of the 'Banque' was rigidly established, and never permitted to exceed seven per cent. in the aggregate. As before remarked, Poker hands must of necessity be measured by an arbitrary standard, for the reason that hands which involve in their drawing similar mathematical difficulties are, when obtained, totally different in value. For instance, it is as hard to draw three Deuces as to draw three Aces, and the value of the latter, it is unnecessary to say, is infinitely superior to the former. Hence each hand has to be equated, in accordance with the standard erected to determine its relative value, and the results arrived at may be considered, for all practicable purposes, sufficiently accurate.

We have no disposition to complicate the volume with needless dissertations on mathematical niceties; our object is to give results in as few words as possible. We think, however, that the reader should be made acquainted with the principle upon which the calculations are based, and a simple problem will illustrate it. Suppose a full pack of cards is thoroughly shuffled and five cards are dealt you, which consist for instance, of four Hearts and a card of an odd suit. Your object is to make a flush of hearts, and you discard the odd suit and draw a fresh card from the pack. Now, before seeing the fresh card, you wish to determine what your chance of making the flush is. You know of course that you hold four hearts in your hand, and that there are nine others among the 47 cards which remain in the pack. It is clear then that your chance is as 9 to 47, which would be 5 2-9 to 1 against your making it. Although in this illustration there is but one hand dealt, *it is immaterial how many hands are dealt*, the *chance* remaining always the same. This we will illustrate in the following example: let five cards be dealt to you from a full pack; let us assume that three of them are Aces, and that you discard the two odd cards and draw two fresh ones from the pack, and that before seeing them you calculate the chances of getting in another Ace in the draw. It is certain that the fourth Ace is among the forty-seven cards that remain in the pack, and that the two cards you draw entitle you to 2:47 of the certainty. It is therefore 23½ to 1 against your drawing it. This is indisputable. Now suppose that five others are playing with you, all of whom agree to remain "in," and, that they discard and receive ten cards among them, making thirty-five cards which they have taken from the 47, let us see if your chance of drawing the fourth Ace is changed in the least. As they have had 35 of the 47 cards which contain the Ace, it is 35:47 that some one of them has received it. It is, on the other hand, 12:47 that none of them has received it, and that it remains in the pack, from which you are to draw two cards. As there are but twelve left, your chance of drawing it is therefore 2:12. Hence 2:12×12:47 (the chance that the other players have not drawn it,) =24:564=1:23½, as originally calculated. It may then be set down as an axiom that the *number* of *players* is a neutral element which determines nothing, and that the reasoning must be based on the five cards which you receive and know and the 47 which are unknown.

The rules for the government of the game, which conclude the volume, have been carefully revised and adapted to meet modern requirements. Many of those now in force are simply preposterous, and are evidently the threadbare ones which formerly applied to "Straight-Poker," now obsolete. Of course the enforcement of rules depends upon the players themselves; and as Poker parties are not slow to eliminate any discordant element that may appear in their midst, it is to be presumed that a conscientious interpretation will be placed upon the construction of the Rules and Laws herewith submitted. This conceded, and the stake at issue confined to moderate limits, Draw-Poker will hold its prominence as a game while cards exist.

DRAW-POKER.

Chapter I.

The game of Draw-Poker is, perhaps, the most fascinating one played with Cards. The innumerable combinations that present themselves, the rapid changes, and that never failing spring, which Hope ever supplies so bountifully with the nectar of the future,—all tend to make it pre-eminently the game of games.

Apart from the cards which the players may hold, whether good or bad is, at times, of no consequence, a thorough exhibition of each individual character is revealed at every step of the game, and even the most casual observer cannot help perceiving that the commodity known as *selfishness* predominates to an unlimited degree, notwithstanding the various contrivances the players adopt to conceal its presence. Possibly this selfish element may be one of its charms. It is certainly an evidence that each player is so warmly interested in the results of the game, that the chances of his falling asleep, during its progress, are so remote that they are not worth considering. Indeed it will be found not only a selfish game, but one that every subterfuge that can be brought to bear is introduced; every artifice that the laws of the game will permit, is pressed into service; and all directed at one object, viz:—to win your money. To the majority of players it requires no ghost to tell them all this; they will, however, one and all, vouch for its truth. Yet there are a large and growing number of young men, novices at the game, who imagine that they can play it for amusement, like whist and euchre, and confine their losses to a trifling amount. Such is not the case. Draw-Poker is strictly a gambling game, and one which, if they will take the author's advice, they will shun as they would a faro-table or a horse-race.

If they have never indulged in the game, they are earnestly exhorted at this point to seek no further information, but to remain happy in their innocence, with the assurance that their position in society will not be imperilled in the least by their ignorance of this accomplishment.

It is unnecessary to say that the game should never be permitted to enter the family circle, no matter how trifling the stake proposed may be.

To those, however, who have played the game and intend to play it, the author has endeavored to point out all that experience on one hand, and mathematical analysis on the other, can do to protect them from the wary adversary, whose insatiable appetite for gain is only stimulated by each success.

The first great requisite in sitting down to play the game is, that during its progress you permit nothing to escape your observation. If you are in doubt, at any period of the play, as to the number of cards any particular player took, you may be certain that you have been indifferent to this rule, and must under no circumstances allow yourself to be placed at a disadvantage a second time. You must not only remember the number of cards each player draws, but endeavor to study his style of drawing, which, with a little attention to the hands that are shown, you can readily acquire. You will find, for instance, in the course of the game, a player frequently drawing two cards, and not having improved his hand, throwing it up. You must assume that he drew to a "bob-tail" flush. Another will draw one card, and when the hand is shown, will be found to have "three-of-a-kind." But it is useless at this juncture to say more, as we shall have all such illustrations presented in their due order and proper place, and will only repeat, to impress upon the reader, the importance of the assertion, that the first great requisite, in playing the game of Draw-Poker is to permit nothing to escape your observation.

The next point of importance to be considered is the kind of players that compose your party. The respective temperament of each player is admirably brought out in the progress of the game, so that you can classify it with as much certainty as an experienced botanist can determine the character and quality of a plant that is presented for his inspection. Poker parties, as a rule, consist of three elements: the close player, the conservative player, and the reckless player. In a party of six, you will be likely to find two of the first, three of the second, and one of the third.

The close player is one who rarely "bluffs." He is content to wait patiently until he gets a good hand, and then bets with almost a certainty of winning. No matter how good his hand may be, he will not venture beyond a certain point, thereby escaping large losses, should an extraordinary hand be opposed to him. At the end of the game he is usually a small winner. His style of play, however, is not to be commended, as it is tedious and uninteresting, and can afford but little pleasure.

The conservative player is one who adapts himself to circumstances; he plays a close or a conservative, or even a reckless game if he feels that the conditions warrant it. He knows the value of his own hand, and anticipates that of his opponent. He is familiar with every movement that has been made during the deal,—knows the number of cards each one has drawn—whether there was any nervousness or hesitancy exhibited—how any certain player is betting, and if it is unusual—if he is a close player or a reckless one—if he has been in good luck or otherwise; these points, and others that may have presented themselves to him, are quickly summed up, and he governs himself accordingly. If he still feels confidence in his hand, and he perceives an indication of wavering in his antagonist, he presses him without mercy; but if, on the contrary, he finds himself in error he "drops" instantly. (The distinguishing trait of a good Poker player is, that he can check himself at once. A poor one is stubborn, and permits his pride to carry him on, even at times when he feels morally certain that he is throwing his money away.)

The reckless player is one who is infatuated with the game, and never permits an opportunity of bluffing to go by without indulging in it. Give him a good pair, or "four-flush," and he will raise the "blind" to the limit. Should he improve his hand in the draw, he will bet it far above its value. At times he will appear to have every thing his own way; but in the long run he is always a loser. His only chance of success is with players reckless like himself; all others are obnoxious to him.

Draw-Poker, like every other game of chance, is based, more or less, upon mathematical deduction, in which the theory of probabilities plays an important part.

We find, by every day observation, that whenever an event of one kind happens permanently more often than one of another kind, there exists some reason for such frequency of occurrence, which, had it been inquired into before any event happened, would have enabled us to predict the frequency in question. So much is this the case, that if we were to take an observer to an urn in which were black and white balls, but how many of each he is not told, and were to make 1000 drawings, replacing the ball drawn after each drawing, and shaking the urn before every trial; if of the 1000 drawings 822 were white and 178 black, he would be irresistibly led to conclude that there must be more white balls than black ones in the urn. More than this, a person used to observation would conclude, not only that there are more white balls in the urn, but that the proportion of white and black balls does not differ very greatly from that of 822 to 178. Suppose a box to contain 3 white, and 4 black balls; it is easily admitted that it is more likely that a black ball should be drawn than a white one, on the supposition that the drawer does not see the balls. Or rather we should say it is easily admitted that every well regulated mind *ought* to think a black ball more likely than a white one: and that if any should imagine the contrary, he has formed an opinion from prejudice, fancy, or want of proper consideration.

Those who cultivated games of chance must at all times have had a general notion of combinations which were more probable than others, and must have seen that those cases of which there were most to happen, always did in reality happen most often. They could not fail to know, by reckoning on their fingers, that out of, for instance, all the throws of a pair of dice, there are only six doublets, and thirty other equally possible cases; nor could they have missed knowing that this must be the reason why doublets occur seldom in comparison with other throws. Notwithstanding the simple nature of such problems, it is admitted, that there are no questions in the whole range of applied mathematics which require such close attention, and in which it is so difficult to escape error, as those which occur in the theory of probabilities. And of all subjects, there is no one in which writers of every grade have so frequently or so strangely made mistakes of mere inadvertence. Cardan's numerical reasoning on certain throws of dice is totally false. Poisson, and even the great Laplace, have been called to account for errors committed.

To Laplace, however, we are indebted for his great work, which gives at one view the whole state of the science and its applications, particularly to Life Annuities and Life Insurance, etc.

These formulas are applicable to all games of chance, in which the conditions are clearly defined; Draw-Poker, from the fact that the bluffing element is fictitious, and the winning hand variable, presents insuperable difficulties in a mathematical point of view; yet the calculations herewith introduced, will be found to cover every point of interest in the game, and are not only correct in their general results, but entirely original in their application.

It will be proper, perhaps, at this point, to dwell a moment in considering the part that "*luck*" plays in the question of probabilities.

Mathematically speaking, there is no such thing as luck; and if it were possible to expunge the word and its several definitions from all the vocabularies in existence, mankind would be a decided gainer by the act. It is the universal *ignis fatuus* that has lured millions into the quagmires of destruction. Ever put forward by the idle and incompetent to excuse and palliate their short-comings; and it has never been known to aid its votaries at the critical moment of their existence. To the beggar, and to the King, it has proved equally false and illusive; and while it smiles approvingly on 'intelligence', 'perseverance' and 'frugality,' it is prepared to trip them up at the earliest opportunity. It is incredible how completely the masses are held in subjection by its lurid glare, and that even the most improbable event is considered within grasp, when looked at through its medium. Every fruitless attempt to clutch the prize, only stimulates still greater exertions, equally fruitless.

The multifarious schemes of "lotteries," "gift concerns," "faro," and "banque" games generally, owe their existence, and live upon the credulity and stupidity of its followers. The per-centage in favor of these games winning, is enormous. Twenty five per-cent. is considered moderate by the harpies who own them, which is simply robbery. On the Continent, where gaming up to a recent period was legalized, 7½ per cent. was the most allowed the "Banque," and with this, the profits were some seasons fabulous.

To make this question of per-centage clear to the reader, and prove to him that where-ever it exists it must invariably win, I will refer to the experiments of Lacroix. This mathematician was noted for putting his theories, so far as possible, to practical tests. He tossed up a coin 4000 times, and found it came "head" 1982, and "tail" 2018 times. He immediately suspected that there was some difference of weight in favor of the "tail," which proved on inspection to be the fact. He next had two ivory balls made, about the size of marbles, with a black speck in one, to distinguish it from the other. They were precisely of a size and weight, and were revolved in a box made for the purpose, before each drawing. 100,000 drawings were made, with the following results; black was drawn 50,002, and white 49,998 times, thus proving theory and practice, within an infinitesimal fraction identical.

Now suppose for every black ball that was drawn the "Banque" paid one dollar; for every white one that was drawn the "Banque" received one dollar and one cent, which, as per-centage, is extremely small: yet it would be so apparent to the comprehension of every body, that no one would consider himself fool enough to engage in it as a player.

The "Banque" understands this perfectly, and at once makes a "combination" far more palatable to the player, and more profitable to itself. Its manager shakes two dice in a leather cup,—"Now gentlemen, name your 'doublet' one dollar gains you thirty, if you guess the right one." Here the chances are thirty-six to one that the particular doublet named will not come up:—this is twenty per cent. in favor of the "Banque;" illustrated by the ivory balls, before mentioned, would read, for a black ball drawn, "Banque" pays 80 cents; for a white ball drawn, "Banque" receives $1. This is precisely what per-centage means. A combination of three dice however is the usual game played at the present day, and a dollar bet on, for instance, three "sixes," should they turn up, gains $180. This looks very large, and the players imagination conjures up pictures of endless wealth. Yet a mathematical analysis shows that the chances are 216 to 1 against the three "sixes" (or any other three) being thrown. The per-centage, as before, is nearly 20 per cent. against the player. Let us illustrate this so that a person who cannot appreciate 20 per cent. may understand it.

Suppose two persons agree to throw dice, say for a dollar a side each throw; the one who represents the "Banque" has three dice to play with of the usual character; the other, who may be termed the "outsider" has three dice to play with, *each one of which has a blank side*—the 4 is absent, which counts nothing, when it happens to turn up. Each player is to throw his respective dice, and the one having the most points turned up wins the stakes. A few throws will satisfy the "outsider" that he is bound to lose,—indeed the first throw will be sufficient, if the blank side of even one die turn up. His reason at once supplants his imagination.

and he sees that the contest is hopeless. The per-centage in this illustration is precisely the same as where the "Banque" pays 180 for 1, and the players, in either case, will lose in the long run equal amounts.

Chapter II.

We have thus glanced at a few of the applications of the theory of probabilities to matters, not strictly, perhaps, called for in this volume; but the reader will unquestionably derive a benefit from their perusal, as every illustration that bears upon the doctrine of chances, only serves to make clearer to him the important but complicated subject we have undertaken.

We have assumed in starting, that he is no stranger to the game we are about to investigate; that he knows that it is played with a full pack of cards; that he knows a "pair," "two pairs," "three-of-a-kind," a "sequence," a "flush," a "full-hand," "four-of-a-kind," and a "straight-flush," are names given to certain hands which determine, on a call, to whom the stakes shall go; that he knows that the player sitting immediately to the left of the dealer starts the game by anteing a chip, and that the other players are entitled to "come in" by putting two chips in the pool; the first player then puts in an additional chip, so all interested in the hand have deposited in the pool equal sums. He is also aware, that the dealer, in dealing the cards, begins with the player at his left hand, who holds the "age," and gives one at a time alternately, until each player has received five cards. This, which by the way, the reader may not know, is termed the "*original hand.*"

Each player has the right to discard any or all of the original hand, and to receive from the dealer cards equal in number to those so discarded. The hand so amended is termed the "*playing hand.*" Where a player stands "pat," his original hand becomes his playing hand. "Straddling," and raising the "blind," will be referred to in the proper place.

To simplify, as far as possible, the calculations upon which the game is based, six players are supposed to constitute the party, four of whom remain in, two throwing up their cards. This will be found a fair average.

The original hand is now dealt, and four of the six players remain in. The mathematical calculation which proves that the *average* value of the four hands in question consists of a *pair of* 8's, would occupy too much space, and is therefore omitted. A player holding in his original hand a pair of 8's, or better, has a mathematical expectation in the game equal to the stake he has invested in the pool. Of course the reader will understand that we use the term *average* in its strict sense; the four hands here referred to, might each be superior to a pair of 8's in this particular deal; but in a long series of deals it will be found as we have stated. The reader can deduce from this fact, that, in playing a close game to win, it is necessary to have at least a pair of 8's to start with. One of the weak points with young players is their anxiety to be in every time, and of course stand on any pair, frequently on odd cards: but in the long run it is found to be a losing game. The rapidity with which they dispose of their chips is the best evidence of its truth. Where amusement, however, is considered more than chips, the rule should be relaxed, and the player will occasionally draw to a pair of Deuces a hand that sweeps the board. But to return to our starting point. The four original hands now discard, and take in return from the dealer, the number of cards they require. The mathematical calculation shows that the improvement culminates in *two pairs,—Jacks and Sixes.* In other words, the four playing hands turned up and exposed, without bluffing, Jacks and Sixes will be, once in four deals, the winning hand. In this, like all average calculation, none of the four hands may have improved—and again, each of the four may have improved superior to Jacks and Sixes; but in the long run, the result above mentioned will be found strictly accurate.

The advantage the reader derives from this knowledge is not, at a glance, very apparent; but it is sufficient to point out to him the standard by which he can measure the value of his hand—if it is inferior to the average, or superior to the average, and can govern himself accordingly. It also brings up another very important matter, and certainly one which will repay a careful perusal.

Notwithstanding that two pairs—Jacks and Sixes—constitute a full average playing hand, it is almost worthless as an original or pat hand. This sounds paradoxical, but we will endeavor to substantiate it. Two pairs pat, it is no exaggeration to state, has cost the amateur more money, and deceived him more frequently than any other combination in the pack. Let us illustrate this: the four players who remain in the game, have, for instance, the following original hands: Jacks and Sixes; Four-flush; a Straight, open at both ends; and a pair of Queens. The player holding Jacks and Sixes has, it is unnecessary to say, at this point the advantage; but the draw at once reduces it to zero. This will be evident when we consider that to improve his hand at all, he must draw a Jack or a Six, of which there are, in the 47 cards unknown to him, but four; consequently his chance is one in $11\frac{3}{4}$, or nearly 12 to 1 that his hand will not be improved, and as there is no other way by which it can be improved, this chance is absolute. The Four-flush has nine cards to draw from out of the 47 unknown, his chance of filling is 1 in $5\frac{2}{9}$, or a little more than 5 to 1 against him; the Straight, or Sequence, open at both ends, has eight cards to draw from, in the 47 unknown, making his chance of filling 1 in $5\frac{7}{8}$, or a little less than 6 to 1 against him; the pair of Queens draws *three* cards and, as there are two Queens in the 47 unknown cards, his chance of taking in another Queen, is about one chance in 8, or, of course, 8 to 1 against him;—but the Queens may be improved by other cards, and the chances are only 4 to 1 that such will not be the case. Hence it will be noticed, that the combined chances of the three hands make the fourth one, holding Jacks and Sixes, nearly or quite worthless.

Inexperienced players are invariably dazzled on finding two pairs in their original hand; it looks *so large* that they raise the ante to the limit, which is responded to by several players. Mr. Two-pairs draws a card without any improvement to his original hand, but nevertheless feels duty bound to make a demonstration, and bets the limit, which the owner of three Fives accepts, and goes as much better; the countenance of the former shows defeat in every line, but his pride urges him to call, which he does, and therefore loses on every side. Once in twelve times he is entitled to fill—and when he does, and is anxiously suppressing the torrent of vengeance which is oozing out of his finger ends, he finds to his intense disgust, that he has no opponent, "every body out." An experienced player by no means despises two pairs; being his age, with Aces or Kings at the head, he will raise a moderate amount, and if not raised back, will draw one card and bet pretty well up to the limit. If, however, he is raised back, he will consider: if by a close player he will throw his hand up; if by a conservative player, he will stand the raise, and draw one card; if by a reckless player, he will stand the raise, play his hand pat, taking the chances that the reckless player is bluffing. The best players, as before remarked, while they do not despise two pairs, put very little trust in their efficacy, and always treat them as doubtful property.

CHAPTER III.

WE have now arrived at a point where it will be proper perhaps to explain what we understand by "poor original hands." We have before remarked substantially, that the fundamental error of all amateurs is their anxiety to be "in" every hand, notwithstanding the cards to which they are to draw are nearly worthless. It is hardly necessary to say that occasions will at once be recalled by every Poker player, where very large hands were drawn to very poor cards. While admitting this, we are free to say, that more money is chipped away in drawing to frivolous cards than in any other way. We have here tabulated a series of original hands (from which the discards have been made) showing how much the *draw* will add to their value. This calculation is of course based upon an *average* adjustment of all the possible combinations that can be drawn.

STANDING ON.	CARDS DRAWN.	AVERAGE VALUE.
An Ace,	4	pair of 8's.
Ace and King,	3	pair of 8's.
Ace, King and Queen,	2	pair of 5's.
Ace, King, Queen, Jack,	1	pair of 2's.
Four-flush,	1	pair of Jacks.
Three-flush,	2	0.
Four-straight, open,	1	pair of 9's.
Four-straight, closed,	1	pair of 2's.
Pair of Deuces,	3	pair of Jacks.
" Treys,	3	pair of Queens.
" Fours,	3	pair of Kings.
" Fives,	3	pair of Aces.
" Sixes,	3	two pairs, 7's and 2's.
" Sevens,	3	" 9's and 5's.
" Eights,	3	" Jacks and 6's.
" Nines,	3	" Queens and 10's.
" Tens,	3	" Kings and 2's.
" Jacks,	3	" Kings & Queens.
" Queens,	3	" Aces and 3's.
" Kings,	3	" Aces & Queens.
" Aces,	3	Three 2's.

In drawing to small pairs under 5's, it will be well to keep with the pair an Ace, should you have one, and draw two cards. There is a trifle advantage in this, besides it helps to conceal your hand.

Instead of standing on an Ace, as many do, and drawing four cards, it is better to throw up your entire original hand and draw five cards. It is found by experience that the cards can rarely be shuffled so as to separate entirely previous hands, and taking five cards in a lump will sometimes produce an admirable hand.

Starting with Three-of-a-kind in your original hand, you have a decided average advantage in your favor. If it is your age, and therefore last say, you should raise the pool an amount that you think the majority of those in will stand. You must not over-do this, else you may frighten them out. Should you be sitting to the left of the age, and of course your first ante, it will be well to omit the raise, taking the chances of other players doing it, and giving you the opportunity of going over them. In discarding, with such a hand, it is sometimes good policy to keep up an odd card with your triplets, to disguise them, and draw one card. If it is evident, however, from the raising that large hands are out, draw two cards. In the first instance, having triplets with an odd card and drawing one card, your chances are as follows: it is 47 to 1 against your making four-of-a-kind; and it is 16 to 1 against your making a full-hand, making your mathematical expectation, say $\frac{1}{12}$. In the second case, you draw two cards and your chances are as follows: it is 23½ to 1 against your making four-of-a-kind; and it is 12 to 1 against your making a full-hand, your mathematical expectation is therefore $\frac{1}{8}$. Hence the advantage lies with the two card draw. Triplets, Nines and upward, make a strong hand, and must never be abandoned without due consideration. Do not give too much weight to the fact that one of your opponents drew one card, and another two cards; yours is a hand above the average of "threes," and should be played accordingly. Even with three Deuces in your hand, you must reflect before throwing it up.

A Straight, or Sequence is, as the reader is aware, five cards of any suits following consecutively, as Ten, Jack, Queen, King and Ace; the Ace may be reckoned as 1 or as Ace; when as 1, the Straight is one of the smallest: when as Ace, one of the largest; it cannot be reckoned both ways in the same hand. In modern Poker, the Straight is superior to Three-of-a-kind; it is mathematically inferior however, but from the fact that it gives more scope for bluffing, it is permitted to retain this position. Hence when an opponent stands his hand pat, and you have not improved your triplets, it becomes a nice question for you to determine whether he is bluffing or not. You will of course be guided to a certain extent by his antecedents, and if he is in the habit of standing pat on two pairs, or without anything in his hand. Should you have a straight pat, endeavor to get all you can by raising when it is your turn to ante, as you draw no cards, your hand is at once disclosed. A Straight is a very strong hand, and must not be thrown up without a struggle. Having a four-straight the chance of making it, as before mentioned, is about 1 in 6. If but one end only is open, or you require an intermediate card to make it, your chance is about 1 in 12, precisely the same chance that you have in making two pairs a full-hand by drawing one card. It is not judicious, under ordinary circumstances, to split a pair of Nines or upward, to draw for a Straight. Yet, if appearances point at large original hands, and be fore your turn to draw some one stands pat, it will be well, not only to split a pair of Nines, but even a pair of Queens.

The ordinary "Flush" is an interesting hand, not only from the fact that it is really a very strong one, but that it presents at least $\frac{4}{5}$ of itself at the immediate opening of the game, as if it took a personal interest in the proceedings. In this form it is known as four-flush, and is constantly appearing during the game, first in one hand, then in another, but always coquettish in its actions, and requiring a good deal of coaxing to put in an appearance in full costume. Its stubbornness is proverbial; notwithstanding, it performs, in the long run, all that can reasonably be expected of it. Some players imagine that they ought to fill a four-flush nearly every time, which is of course absurd: the chance of filling, as before referred to, is 1 in $5\frac{2}{9}$, and you are entitled to fill twice in eleven times. Occasionally, in a fit of desperation, a player draws on what is known as a "monkey," or "bob-tail" flush, which is three cards of a suit, in expectation that the two cards which he draws will be of the same suit, making a flush. It is sometimes accomplished, but it is an expensive luxury as the chances will show: $4\frac{7}{10}\times5\frac{2}{9}=24\frac{5}{9}$ to 1 against making it. There are some players who always raise the blind on having a four-flush; it is, however, playing against a strong per-centage, and should not be indulged in more than a few times during the game, and then if the hand does not fill, it must be bluffed through, if possible. A pat Flush should be played precisely, as pointed out in the case of the Straight, your chances of winning are however greatly enhanced. When two players stand pat, the one holding a flush has nearly two chances to one of winning the pool, for the reason that for four pat flushes, there are seven pat straights and but one pat full. In splitting pairs above Nines, to draw for a flush, you can risk more than in drawing for a straight, as the flush is easier to make and a stronger hand when made. With but one in besides yourself, unless the blind is raised, stand on Tens in preference to splitting them. But at any time, should you think it necessary, do not hesitate to split even a pair of Aces.

A full hand is a combination that requires but few comments; to have it is to say that the pool is, almost to a certainty, within your grasp. To get it pat, is an occurrence that cannot be expected many times during the game; if you get it twice in that time you are doing well. It must be played cautiously, like all pat hands; you must start with a small raise which, should it be returned, you must repeat. Your opponent will then possibly go the limit, and you can follow suit. But if you go the limit at the first start, you will keep some out who would otherwise venture in on the small raise, and at the same time call attention to your hand. If it is your first bet go the limit, as it may induce some to think you are only bluffing. Should you hold a full, made by standing on one pair, and you are first to bet, go merely a chip; if second, and the first goes a chip, go something over him, (no matter how many are behind you; they may all drop out, or but see the chip) and the first player has then a chance of going you better, which is what you desire; bet quietly at the start, and allow yourself to be drawn gently along, as it were.

We have now glanced at the combinations that usually constitute the ordinary hands at Poker; the few that remain to be considered may be classed as exceptional, as their appearance cannot reasonably be expected, save at long and unequal intervals. Four-of-a-kind is a hand of this description. A gentleman who kept a record for six months at a private club, where the game was played every evening, stated that four-of-a-kind pat occurred, on an average, once in two weeks; that a hand holding "fours" was dealt once every three hours. The chances are as follows: the first card dealt you is, say for instance, an Ace, it is 5202 to 1 that in the next four cards, you do not get three more Aces. It is therefore 5202 to 1 that your original hand will not have fours pat in any particular deal; 867 to 1 that none of the six players will hold fours pat in any particular deal. With two Aces in the original hand, discarding three cards and getting from the dealer three others, the chance of having two more Aces in said three cards is 1 in 364. With three Aces in the original hand, and two cards are drawn, the chance of getting the fourth Ace is 1 in 23½. Of course the same chances apply as well to all other cards as to Aces. Four-of-a-kind pat should be played like all pat hands,—moderately at the start;

if you raise the blind and it is merely seen, draw one card, as if you had two pairs; if there is considerable raising and it is evident that there are good hands out, play your hand pat, and you will get credit for holding a straight, a flush, or a full. Should you stand on a pair, or three-of-a-kind, and make fours, your object will be to conceal as far as possible the strength of your hand, as the ultimate result is almost certain. It will be perceived here, from the calculations made that it is no easy matter to draw four-of-a-kind, and the reader should bear this in mind should he at anytime hold an ace-full.

The Straight, or Sequence Flush, is the final combination in the game, and to which all other hands must bow. Unlike four Aces, which, in ancient Poker, was the highest hand and certain to win, this offers no such advantage, at least in a mathematical point of view, as the four highest may be out in the same deal, and in that case the pool is divided equally among the holders. Although there is no absolute certainty, then, of winning any pool in the game of Draw-Poker, the holder of even the smallest straight-flush may consider his moral claim in the premises pretty sure, as the chances will show: assuming that your first card is an Ace, it is 249,900 to 1, that you will not, in your next four cards draw King, Queen, Jack and Ten of the suit; again, standing on an Ace, it is 124,950 to 1 that you will not make either the highest or lowest straight-flush, in the next four cards you draw. The most favorable way by which this flush can be made is to start on a centre card, say a Seven spot, as you have either side with you; even in this case it is 15,619 to 1 that you will not make it. Suppose you start with a 7 and 8, it is then 2450 to 1 that you will not succeed. Very few players attempt to make a straight-flush without having in their original hand at least a sequence of three cards, say for instance, 7, 8 and 9 of a suit, and the chance of making it is 1 in 275. With a sequence of four cards of a suit in your original hand, your chance of making a straight-flush is not unreasonable, being but 23½ to 1 against you. In this combination, there is the chance to make the ordinary flush, and also to make an ordinary straight, hence its appearance in the hand of a player is hailed with pleasure; its failure to benefit him, however, is expressed in no very flattering terms.

Chapter IV.

The game of Draw-Poker has been very much improved during the past twenty years, and at the present time is unquestionably at the head of all games played with cards. Its lineage may be traced back, without difficulty, to its progenitor, the good old game of "Brag," in which, in former years, many of our great statesmen indulged their propensity "to go better," even if it involved the loss of a small plantation. At the present day the amount at stake at any one time is usually limited to a moderate sum: this is an important feature, as it is a very easy matter, even among friends, to provoke a contest over a game of cards that might result disastrously. But with the amount that can be bet at one time limited, either contestant can bring the issue to a conclusion at once, without much pecuniary sacrifice. Among gentlemen who play the game for amusement the limit is fixed at $2.50 to $5;

in some few cases it will be placed at $10. It will be found that $2.50 is limit large enough to bring out all the pleasure the game is susceptible of, and not unfrequently, even at this small amount, $100 will change hands during an evening. If the reader prefers a large or unlimited game, it is to be presumed that he requires no advice at our hands.

We will now assume that a party is formed, and that six persons sit around a convenient table all anxious to begin "business." Two packs of cards are procured, having backs of different or opposite colors, which are to be dealt alternately; a box of ivory "chips" or counters of three sizes: $2.50, $1, quarter dollar; a package of small blank cards, or any stiff white paper cut up will answer, and a lead pencil or two. The blank cards are for the use of those who may run out of chips and wish to give their neighbor a "coup," representing for the moment a due bill. Each player takes twenty-five dollars worth of chips, say 6, 8, 8, of the respective sizes, which he has to account for, together with any due bills or coups he may have out, at the end of the game. The cards being new require considerable shuffling; which done, cards are dealt around face up, and he who receives the first Jack has the first deal. The pack is shuffled by the dealer and cut, and he proceeds to give each player five cards, one at a time alternately, commencing with his left hand adversary, and ending with himself.

The player who receives the first card dealt, and of course sits immediately to the left of the dealer, holds the "age." This position entitles him to "ante," or as it is better known in modern Poker, to go blind any sum that does not exceed *half* the limit which has been agreed upon. Whatever sum he goes blind must be placed on the table before he sees any of his cards, and usually indeed before any are dealt. No matter whether he wishes to be in or not, the amount of the blind has to remain as a basis for the pool to be played for. The players then in turn, who wish to be in, put into the pool double the amount of the ante, and the age makes his blind "good", so that all will have contributed alike. A system of betting on the original hand, known as "raising the blind," is one of the most interesting features of modern Poker, unknown in the old game, and is often carried to an extreme. Any player, when it is his turn to ante, has the right to raise the blind to the limit; the next can raise him the limit, and so on indefinitely, and before the discards are made and the final cards dealt, even with $2½ limit, it is not unusual to see $50 on the table. Each player who wishes to raise must do so in turn, and all who are interested in the deal, must, as before mentioned, have equal sums in the pool. With a superior original hand it requires some tact to make the most of it. The age in this case is of great advantage, as the holder of it knows how many are in, and can calculate pretty accurately how much of a raise it is judicious to make. Notwithstanding the age belongs to the player on the dealer's left, his neighbor sitting at his left, has the privilege to "straddle" his blind, which then becomes a double blind; this gives the straddler the opportunity to be the last in, he must, however, make the first bet. It is an error to suppose that there is any advantage in having the blind, and it is a still greater error to straddle it; a close player rarely straddles.

In dealing the cards, care should be taken that they are neatly distributed, without showing any of them. Each hand should be a distinct pile in itself, and no player should touch his hand until all the cards are dealt. No better preliminary test of the relative merits of players can be presented than their respective methods of dealing, discarding, and examining hands. The good player when dealing rarely makes a misdeal, but distributes the cards neatly and in proper order. When the hand is finished, he gathers up the cards, shuffles them and places the pack near the player who has next to use them. When playing, he never touches his cards until they are all dealt; he then takes up his hand and determines in an instant what it contains; he is ready to discard the moment his turn comes, and ready to make his bet without any delay. If his hand is not good he announces that he is out, and at once places his cards, without exposing any of them, near the dealer, and without delaying the game in the least. The poor player, on the contrary, deals the cards in a slovenly manner, giving rise to disputes and misdeals; when he examines his hand he appears to be in doubt what it contains, and has to be repeatedly asked what he intends to do; if he has resolved to stay out he still holds on to his cards, often confusing those who are in; he never appears to know when it is his turn to deal or to ante; always appealing to those around him to witness his bad luck;—uproariously elated when he wins a pool, and uproariously depressed when he loses one; he seldom knows the number of cards his antagonist drew; owes small amounts to every body at the table, and disputes about them afterwards. It is unnecessary, perhaps, to tell the reader that if he labors under any one of the foregoing faults, he should abandon it at once.

We will permit the party to proceed with the game, as we wish, for the moment, to discuss a new subject.

JACK-POTS.

We have, as the reader is aware, substituted the term "*Jack*" for that of "Knave," in speaking of that well known card. We have done so in no capricious spirit of innovation, but simply because nine-tenths of those who play Poker designate the card in question by that name. So well established, indeed, has it become, that one of the most important modifications of the game, known as the Jack-pot, is now recognized; and it is determined by the player who holds in his hand a pair of those cards; a few words therefore as to its origin may not be out of place.

In every poker party one or two players are to be found who invariably play an exceedingly close game. Experience having taught them that unless they held fair average original hands their chances of winning were limited. Hence these gentlemen never came in unless they held the requisite cards. This, of course, did not infringe any rule of the game; still it was not calculated to make an harmonious party, especially at times when a liberal player was obliged to throw up good hands for want of opponents. It was suggested that some method should be devised to compel every player to contribute at intervals to the pool, whether his hand warranted it or not, and the Jack-pot was the result, and it has been found in many cases to equalize the players admirably.

There are two ways of playing it: one is the simple Jack-pot; the other the graduated one. In the former a chip is put in the pool by each player until some one holds a pair of Jacks, or better, in his original hand, and announces that he will "open" it; the game then assumes its usual character.

The graduated Jack-pot is more elaborate, and frequently contains a large amount of chips. Each player, as in the former case, puts a chip in the pool, and if no one holds a pair of Jacks, or better, in his original hand, the cards are dealt again, each putting in a chip as before; this time it requires a pair of Queens, or better; if not opened, the next deal requires a pair of Kings, or better, and finally a pair of Aces, or better. It remains at Aces until it is opened, and, as before stated, as each one puts a chip in each deal, the pool is often very large and usually gives rise to a warm contest. When it is opened, that is to say, when a player announces that he has the required cards in his hand, and fixes the amount at which it is to be opened, any, or all the other players at the table can come in, no matter what they may hold in their hands, and can even raise the party opening it if they wish. After the discards are made, the player who opened it must make the first bet and show, if he is not called, the cards with which he opened the pot.

Jack-pots afford unusual scope for finessing and bluffing, and are frequently made a feature of the game towards its close. A vigorous style of play is essential, else you will see pot after pot go to the reckless player. With a strong hand, it will be well to open it for an amount that will induce everybody to be in ; with a hand just sufficient to open it, make it the limit to come in and draw one, or two cards, and bet the limit : by these means you will keep some out, and intimidate those who re. main in.

A great error is made by many persons in their method of playing Jack-pots. The rule they lay down is this: "any player having the required hand *must open it.*" Now Poker is a game in which no one is obliged to play his hand unless he wishes to do so, and by adopting the above rule you change entirely its spirit and policy. The object of this pot is to increase the pool, so that it will be of substantial value to the individual who may win it ;

hence the conditions of opening it, or not, may be left untrammelled with the players, self interest being quite sufficient in all such cases. Therefore the rule should be, any player holding the necessary hand, beginning with the one at the dealer's left, the dealer himself having the last say, *may* open the "pot;" It is the dealer's business to ask each one in turn, "will you open it:" if the response is "no," he passes to the next; if a player says "no," and wishes to withdraw it, he should do so at once, and before the next one answers, else he will be obliged to pass out. Any one opening it all can come in, after putting up the required amount. Many good players have adopted this method, with entire satisfaction. It will be perceived that there is nothing obligatory whatever. If you have the necessary hand you can open, or not, as you think proper. But if you have the cards with which you can open it and fail to do so, taking the chances that some one else will do it, you cannot be permitted to avail yourself of the privilege when you see that all the players are about to pass out. Each one should therefore examine his hand carefully, and say "yes," or "no," understandingly, and the rule should be strictly enforced.

Jack-pots are usually introduced when a mis-deal occurs, or when all the players pass out of a hand. Frequently the game terminates with a series of such pots.

Chapter V.

Our party of six have now brought their game to a close, and a commentary on what may be termed "good play," and its opposite, or "bad play," will convey to the reader all that can be properly set forth in an elementary work of this description. There is no royal road to successful poker playing, unless we pave the way ourselves: coolness, patience, sagacity and tact being essential in its construction.

The fundamental error of the "bad player," (who is the representative of bad playing generally,) has been mentioned repeatedly; he wants to be in every hand, and to do so, he stands on bob-tail flushes, intermediate straights, and odd cards. Once in, he will stand a raise on the cards just mentioned. Now if one will reflect a moment on the absurdity of this course, he must see that it is almost impossible to win under the circumstances. Thirty-three per-cent. of all the hands dealt are mathematically worthless, hence it is easy to calculate the amount of money thus thrown away. A further illustration may be found by inspecting the "widow," which receives a chip at a time, and at the end of the game will be found one of the chief winners. It may be set down as a rule that losses at Poker, where the game is limited, result almost entirely from standing on inadequate original hands. This being admitted, it will be necessary to call attention to an error which even good players make, viz: bet their hands for more than their value. With these two points guarded, the rest of the game will play itself. Of course it is not easy at all times to determine the value of what is usually termed a good hand. Take, for example, an unlooked-for-hand, which is one that is sometimes drawn to odd cards. A player, for instance, stands on an Ace and King, and draws in two more Aces. Now the point of this is that he will bet twice as much on it as if he had had it pat. He is surprised at receiving it and bets it far above its value before he can check himself. In like manner, when your opponent proposes to divide the pot with you, which is a subterfuge on his part, you will of course refuse, having a good pair in your hand; he will then bet you the limit, and you will be induced not only to call him, but frequently to raise him several times, his hand, on being shown, proving far superior to yours.

It would be tedious, perhaps, to dwell upon the thousand-and-one peculiarities that are to be found from time to time in poker playing. Each player has a certain idiosyncrasy peculiar to himself, which no language can convey to a reader, and to be studied to advantage must be studied over the cards. With the principal points of the game clearly defined and under. stood, the ability to determine the delicate pencilling that marks its subtile organism will quickly follow.

In concluding this part of our subject, we must call attention to the "good player," and point out some of his characteristic actions, while engaged in playing the game. To start with, he will not play where the limit exceeds five dollars; he never antes, when it is his blind, more than a chip; he will never straddle the blind; he never stands on less than a pair of Sixes in his original hand, except it is his blind; he considers a "four-flush" equal to a pair of Tens, and a four-straight equal to a pair of Sevens, and plays them accordingly, as circumstances may suggest; he is always doubtful of two pairs, and does not take much stock even in threes, unless pretty large. He plays a defénsive game generally and considers the secret of winning to consist of husbanding your chips and betting even strong hands moderately. He does not like Jack-pots, but of course plays them. Notwithstanding the almost adamantine rules with which he governs his play, he appears to be in as often as anybody at the table; bluffs occasionally but effectively, and never shows his hand except he is obliged to. When he bluffs, he selects a time when the player who has the last say is of the weak-kneed order. He prides himself upon the suavity with which he can lay down a good hand, when he feels that he is overmatched, and also upon the many variations he introduces in his style of play, to prevent its becoming at all familiar to his opponents. Now if success is the criterion of good play, then his style is perfection, for he leaves off nineteen times out of twenty a winner, and when he does lose, the amount is insignificant.

Poker limited to $2,50, or even $5, will be

pooh-poohed by many who consider it, when so restricted, beneath their notice. They want an unlimited game where, according to their story, pluck and science are brought into play.

The truth is, there is no science whatever necessary in the unlimited game; it is purely a question of intimidation. The limited game, on the contrary, is highly scientific. Every bet made is liable to be called; therefore a thorough knowledge of all the various combinations that go to make up Poker hands is absolutely essential. To be a successful player, competent to defend yourself against all comers, you must be able to determine quickly and accurately, from the conditions presented, the results likely to be attained; and while of course infallibility is not to be mentioned in connection with a game of chance, the law of per-centage invariably decides in favor of those who comply with its statutes.

We have now examined all the points that have a bearing, remotely or otherwise, upon the game of Draw-Poker. In our discussion, we have not been unmindful of the old adage, "Wise men often allow themselves to be taught many things which they know." A proficient in the game will see the application of the maxim. Every poker player, however, is not a proficient. On the contrary, considering that it is played in all sections of the country, there is really less known about it than almost any other game. A knowledge of the several combinations by which the value of the hand is computed, is not sufficient to make an accomplished player. It is the first step, however, and an important one. To be able to read the actions and expressions of your opponent, and at the same time mask your own, is a step in advance of the former, and equally important.

We mentioned in the earlier part of the volume the importance of studying each opponent's style of play, and the manner in which he acts under the various circumstances that present themselves during the game. It will be found that a large majority of the players, if carefully scrutinized, give certain indications, unconsciously on their part, no doubt, which, almost to a certainty, disclose the character of their hands. Then there will be found those who always bet according to a scale, determined by the cards they hold, and who may be termed stereotyped players; and as they rarely venture to bluff, the strength of their hands, is quickly discovered. While you must avail yourself of every trifle that may in any way tend to your benefit, you should be extremely cautious not to permit the faintest glimmer of your intentions (if the expression may be allowed,) to reach your opponents. Some players, indeed, are so constituted that they find an extreme difficulty in controlling themselves when they get a large hand; and, as this is instantly noticed, they labor under a serious disadvantage as a consequence. It is impossible to be perfect in the game, unless you have absolute command of yourself, under all circumstances. A very great advantage is gained by accustoming yourself to examine your original hand at a glance, as it were, the moment you raise it; and never dwell upon it a second more than is necessary. When you receive the draw, glance at it as you take it up, and direct your attention elsewhere; you will find time enough to re-examine it. This rapidity on your part gives time to prepare yourself, and also to study your opponents. In your manner, always treat a hand that you intend to throw up when your turn comes, precisely as you would one with which you expect to win the pot. The expression of your countenance must not exhibit too much anxiety; but rather partake of what Mr. Swiveller had the happy faculty of putting on, when things with him were about to culminate, "an extremely careful assumption of extreme carelessness."

It may not be out of place at this point to say a word regarding the ethics of the game; indeed it is not certain but that a chapter could be written to advantage on the subject. We must, however, be brief.

In playing the game of Poker, (or indeed any game,) always control your temper; never permit it to gain the slightest ascendency over you. Win and lose with equanimity. Nothing can be more childish than the ebullition of boisterous gratification exhibited by a player who wins a large pot, except, indeed, it be his silly, melancholy whine, when he loses one. Poker, to say the least, is a manly game, and should be played in a manly way. One who cannot meet its losses without losing his temper should never play it.

Do not owe anything around the table; settle at once, if you have anything pending, the moment the hand is played, and exact like treatment from your opponents. Should it occur, that at the close of the game you find yourself indebted to some one of the party a sum that, at the moment, you cannot liquidate; —then do so the next day, without fail. If you find this course does not agree with your purse, give up playing the game.

Never induce anybody to play whose position, financially or otherwise, is not calculated to sustain the expensive amusement that Poker sometimes proves itself to be.

Before taking final leave of our readers, we feel justified in calling their attention to a matter which each one should consider personal to himself, and use his exertions to modify it, if it cannot be entirely removed. We refer to the protraction of the game, long after the hour agreed upon at the start that it should close. This has become so intolerable, that every player who considers self respect an element in matters of recreation, should set his face against it. It is useless, of course, to lay down any rule in such cases; the good sense of the players must be called out for common protection, and then it is to be hoped that this serious evil will disappear. Each player, then, should resolve to stop at the appointed time, no matter how blandly the "*just once around*" is urged, and should feel it to be a personal duty to carry out his part of the contract.

CHAPTER VI.

LAWS AND RULES.

THE laws and rules constructed to govern any game should be few and simple, and as equitable as the conditions will permit. Many of those now in use which relate to Draw-Poker are, however, contradictory in their character, and embarrass players who endeavor to comply with them.

We do not propose to insert in this volume rules that are now acknowledged and assented to by every one who ever played Draw-Poker. We have assumed that the reader knows that a full pack of cards is used in the game; that five cards are dealt to each player, one at a time alternately, commencing with the player immediately to the left of the dealer; that the deal passes to the left, and each player takes it in turn; that the cards must be shuffled above the table, that each player has the right, after placing the required chips in the pool, to discard any or all of his original cards and receive an equal number from the dealer; that when a bet is made the next player must respond, or pass out; that the age, or eldest hand, is entitled to the pool, if no bet is made after the draw; that each player must keep his hand on, or above the table; that on a call, each player must show his hand to the board, and that the best poker hand wins, even if its holder mis-called it; that the player to the left of the age may straddle it, and the player next to him double straddle it, and so on; that if the player entitled to make the first straddle decline it, none can take place that hand; that the age has the last say, and passes to the left, if the original holder announces himself out.

In many sections of the country rules are to be found somewhat different from any we have here. But really this is of no consequence, provided that those they have are equitable, and that the players are aware of their existence. So long as all at the table agree that certain conditions shall govern, no trouble can arise. But the difficulty to be apprehended lies in the fact that some unusual circumstance may occur, in which a rule may be construed to suit a certain contingency, to the detriment of some particular player. Every party, then, should announce before beginning the game the precise rules under which they expect to act.

We wish to consider but a few, which have been variously interpreted, and remain at the present day unsettled.

Rule 1.

The deal is determined by throwing cards around, face up, to each player, and he who receives the first Jack has the first deal.

[The first deal is a matter of no consequence; but the object of determining it by a certain card, which may require a quarter of the pack to be exposed before it appears, is not without a purpose. The dealer sees from the manner in which the cards run, the extent of shuffling they require; and the trifle delay gives the players an opportunity of seating themselves properly at the table.]

Rule 2.—The Dealer.

The dealer has certain duties to perform, the enforcement of which, to a certain extent, is incumbent on the entire board. He must have his cards properly shuffled and cut; and he must deal to each player five cards, one at a time alternately, without exposing any of them.

1. Should he, in dealing, expose a player's card, the player may take it or reject it, at his option, if he has not raised his other cards.

2. Should he deal a player more or less than five cards, the player may demand that cards be added to or taken from his hand, whether he has raised his cards or not, or demand a new deal, at his option.

[It will be perceived that the entire board is interested in this rule, as it gives the player a nominal advantage. Notwithstanding, it is strictly just. The old rule that obliged the player to discover the *dealer's error* before the cards were raised, was illogical. Each player is entitled to five cards; should he find more than five in his hand, he might, under the old rule, be induced to dissemble rather than be thrown out of the hand, and discard more than he intended to draw, without calling attention to the error. And, besides, it places the player at the mercy of the dealer, as it is impossible at all times to tell the number of cards dealt you until the hand is raised.]

3. The card or cards drawn from a hand which contains too many, must be placed at the bottom of the pack. The card or cards added to a hand which contains too few, must be dealt from the top of the pack.

4. After the *discards are made*, should the dealer expose any card or cards of the draw, in dealing them to the player, he must

place the exposed card or cards at the bottom of the pack, continue to supply in turn the rest of the party, and then return to the player whose cards were thus exposed and supply him. Should the player, however, expose his cards by accident, or otherwise, after receiving them from the dealer, he must keep them.

[The players are entitled to the cards that would naturally fall to them, if no accident occurred; and it is justly claimed that the diversion should effect only the hand that caused it, and not extend to any other interested in the pot.]

5. The dealer must announce the number of cards he is about to draw to complete his own hand, and he must take them, if he has set them apart for that purpose. Having once announced the number of cards he has drawn, he is not obliged to repeat it; nor is he allowed to tell the number of cards any other player has drawn.

It ought to be noticed perhaps that formerly the dealer paid a chip for the privilege of dealing, such chip forming the basis of the pot. At the present day, however, this course is not adopted. The player sitting to the left of the dealer, who *always* holds the age, *must* start the game by placing at *least* one chip on the table, which becomes the nucleus of the pot and the property of the board. This amount is termed the "blind," and may consist of one chip up to half the limit.

Rule 3.—The Player.

The player has certain duties to perform, which must be strictly enforced.

1. He must not raise his cards until they are all dealt. Should he do so, he is obliged to accept any card, even an exposed one, that may be dealt him.

2. After he discards, he is responsible for the number of cards which he receives from the dealer; should he raise them and find more or less than he called for, making more or less than five cards in his hand, he forfeits all his interest in that deal to the board. Should he discover the error before raising his cards, the dealer is obliged to correct it, and give to or take from the draw such card as in his judgment is the correct one.

3. When he passes out of a hand, he must at once throw up his cards, without exposing any of them, and he must not make any remark cal-

culated to influence the other players. After his hand has been thrown up, he cannot recall it.

4. All antes, straddles, and bets must be made in chips and placed in the pool. Should he fill his blind at the start, and not wish to come in, throwing up his cards and not drawing any, he is entitled to withdraw half of it.

Rule 4.—Foul Hand.

A foul hand, which is one that does not contain precisely five cards, cannot win, no matter what the circumstances may be, and the pot must be given to the best poker hand among the remaining contestants.

Should it occur that on the call of hands, a foul hand is the only one that is shown, the others having been thrown up, the entire pot remains the property of the table, to be played for and determined the next hand, in the usual way, and the double pot thus created goes to the winner of it.

[The old rule that allowed the foul hand to win the pot, when the other hands had been thrown up, is pernicious in the extreme. It is not based upon either equity or reason, as it evidently permits the holder of it to be benefited by his own wrong, contrary to the spirit of all law, written or otherwise.]

Rule 5.—Value of Hands.

Hands are determined by the highest cards; the highest Pair; the highest two Pairs; the highest Triplets; the highest Straight: Ace and King being in the highest, and Ace and Deuce in the lowest; the highest Flush; the highest Full-hand (the threes of which determine); the highest Fours; the highest Straight-flush. The Ace is always high, except in the lowest Straight, where it is reckoned as One; the King is next; and Queen, Jack, down to Deuce, follow consecutively.

All ties are decided by the highest odd card or cards. Should the hands be an exact tie the pool must be equally divided between them.

Rule 6.—The Stake.

The stake, or amount of chips, taken by each player, must be paid for at the time, and the money placed in the chip-box, which should be in charge of one of the players. When the hour arrives that has been mutually agreed upon at which the game is to end, any player has the right to demand the redemption of any chips which he may hold.

Any unsettled indebtedness that may have been created between players during the game, must be satisfactorily arranged at its close.

[Modern Poker, with all its pleasures, has brought with it in its train, one very objectionable feature. We mean the credit system. To make rules for its adjustment, satisfactory both to winner and loser, would require the genius of Micawber; and even that gentleman would find at times his creative power taxed to an unusual extent.

The credit system originated in the idea that some one of the players could get along without using any money during the game. Each one of course imagined himself to be the favored person, and took a certain amount of chips out of the box as his stake, merely as a matter of form, agreeing to return them at the close of the game. Well, at the termination of the play, the fortunate player found himself, as he predicted, a winner, and the labor and annoyance of paying for his chips at the start, were thus saved. *If* each of the others had fared as well, there could be no objection raised against the system; indeed it would be perfect. But, unfortunately, in this important particular, it has invariably failed. We must therefore class it among certain problems, in which *if* is an important element, and if it could be but eliminated all would be well.

Some improvement in the matter of borrowing chips became necessary when the box was found to be exhausted, and a gentleman hit upon the happy expedient of making and issuing paper due bills, representing certain sums for which he was personally responsible. These issues passed freely from hand to hand, and for a time gave promise of a happy solution of the entire difficulty. But when the game came to an end, the old trouble appeared, and money was found to be as necessary as ever.

The issue of due-bills was not original with our friend the poker player. Mr. William Patterson, who organized the Bank of England in 1694, was unquestionably ahead of him, and extended the promise-to-pay system to its supposed utmost limit. It may be remarked, that even Mr. Patterson found some difficulty in convincing unreasonable people that one issue could be redeemed out of the proceeds of another, without impairing the value of either. But in the end, it was found that a certain quantity of money was absolutely necessary, to make the scheme perfect.

Since Mr. Patterson's time, however, many great improvements have been introduced in his system; and at the present day, among ourselves, an experiment of gigantic proportions is in full blast, in which the highest tribunal of the land has enacted that a piece of paper shall possess a positive and intrinsic value, and that the quantity of it which may be issued, shall in no wise circumscribe or retard its functions as a money.

In this experiment, as printing presses and paper are the only expenditures necessary, it is expected that great national prosperity will follow in its wake. If it prove itself a success, the legal luminaries who invented the process are expected to immediately set about repairing and altering a few of the more obsolete laws of the planetary system, which, in their present state, do not appear to benefit anybody.

But to return to poker credit. It is perfectly clear that, as the players cannot avail themselves of the national prerogative to laugh at their creditors, they must pay up or be disgraced. Hence no one should play who is not prepared to settle his losses at the end of the game, or within a reasonable time thereafter; and that a stringent rule, tacitly acknowledged by all, making a player with outstanding poker indebtedness ineligible to play with the party, should be adopted and enforced.]

Rule 7.—Custom.

Should any dispute arise in determining the value of any particular hand, or any particular method of play, in a party of gentlemen who usually play together, the decision must be in accordance with the precedents which they have established in similar cases, and a majority of those in the game should so decide it.

We must now bring this lit[illegible]to a close. We offer no apology for [illegible]ce; nor do we wish to hint that it [illegible]edly written, without any view to publi[illegible] The latter indeed was an after-thought.

It was discovered by Dr. Johnson t[illegible] works not written to be published, were, nevertheless, published to be read. And so (if a slip or two in orthography, and the eccentricity of a few punctuation points be pardoned) we will say no more on that head.

The morality of card-playing has been a fruitful theme for discussion. We do not propose to enter the lists. Those who have winked at it, and those who have denounced it, may both be in the wrong. It must be admitted, however, by its most bitter enemy that, as a source of recreation, when moderately indulged in, and stripped of its objectionable features, it presents advantages not to be obtained in any other amusement.

THE END.

www.ingramcontent.com/pod-product-compliance
Lightning Source LLC
Chambersburg PA
CBHW020241090426
42735CB00010B/1789
* 9 7 8 3 3 3 7 2 6 6 5 9 2 *